# HUBERTA
## the Hiking Hippo

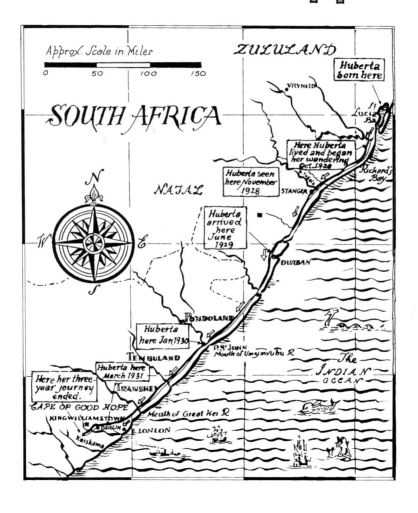

Written by Daphne Cox   Based on a True Story
Illustrated by Melissa Webb

A wild hippopotamus isn't the sort of animal that you expect to become famous. Hippos much prefer quiet lives, wallowing happily with other hippos in the mud of a peaceful waterhole and never venturing far from home.

But in October 1928, in South Africa,
one history-making hippo gave up her
quiet life and began an amazing
three-year journey. It was to be a
journey of frequent surprises — and
not only for the hippopotamus!

Huberta, as the hiking hippo came to be known, probably didn't mean to attract attention. But she could hardly go unnoticed when she did things such as taking a huge bite out of a family's hut in the middle of the night.

She calmly lumbered away, munching
on a mouthful of reeds, as the hut
collapsed behind her. This happened in
November, near a town named Stanger;
it was also in November that some
surprised farmers saw a hippo raiding
their fields of freshly cut sugar cane.

Whether she liked it or not, Huberta was already becoming well known, and more and more people wanted to catch a glimpse of her. Even near small townships she had to spend a lot of time hiding from curious crowds.

When the people didn't go away,
Huberta did. She journeyed farther and
farther south, to the Umvoti River
and beyond.

She did make occasional detours on the way, to visit farms for a snack of sugar cane or cabbage, but she kept mostly to marshes and fields.

Yet even these out-of-the-way places provided some unexpected encounters, especially on the evening when Huberta came upon an open-air rehearsal of the Beulah Society of Bantu Bandsmen. It's hard to say whether Huberta or the musicians got the bigger surprise!

Huberta didn't wait to hear the band's
big concert a few days later. On she
went, and by June 1929 (eight months
after the start of her journey), she had
reached the very large town of Durban.

Residents of this city were treated to
the sight of a hippo in the yard of a
police station, roaming around the
grounds of an exclusive club, and gazing
out to sea from the sandy ocean front.

For some months after this, there was no news at all of Huberta. Then one night (actually it was three o'clock in the morning!) she was seen in the town of Port St. John. She'd discovered that the town's market square made a very tasty grazing patch.

News of Huberta was reported to city officials, and the next night the whole town council was in the square waiting for her. She took immediate action to protect her grazing rights!

But Huberta didn't know just how persistent people could be. When she returned the next night, spotlights and car headlights were suddenly turned on. Half the town had been holding its breath, waiting for her in the darkness.

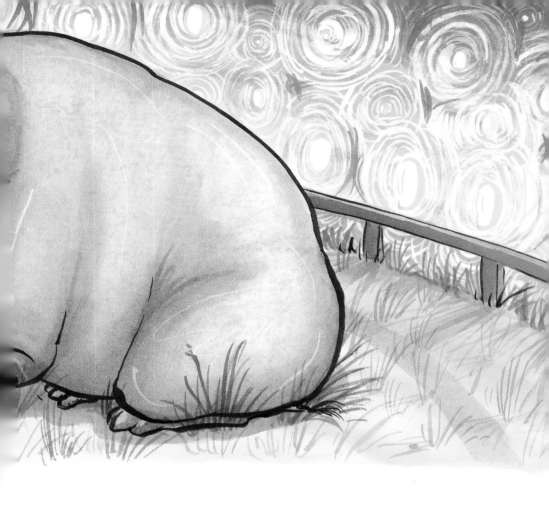

This time Huberta just sat down on
her haunches and stared about her.
Then, heaving herself up, she
lumbered away from the square and
left Port St. John behind her forever.
Again Huberta slipped away.

And this time she stayed out of sight
for so long that people began to think
she must have returned to the wild.
Then, one night in March 1931,
100 miles south of Port St. John,
a freight train was steaming its way
toward Kingwilliamstown.

Suddenly the engineer saw a bulky shape on the tracks ahead, spotlit by his headlamp. It was Huberta, sound asleep. Despite all the train's clanging and hooting and squealing of brakes, she showed no signs of waking up. The engineer was able to slow down just in time.

He nudged Huberta with the
"cow-catcher" on the front of the train,
and this bump finally roused her.
She trotted away into the night.

As always, news of Huberta spread
quickly. This time, however, not
everyone was willing to let her
disappear again.

Now that the hiking hippo was so famous, some people began to think that they could make a lot of money by capturing her and putting her on show. Yet not even the most determined hunters were able to capture Huberta.

They searched for months, but the big, bulky animal somehow hid her trail so well that they didn't even catch sight of her.

How Huberta eluded her hunters nobody will ever know.

Nor will anyone ever really know why Huberta gave up the safety of her home in the first place, to begin a trek that stretched over three years and more than 600 miles.

But there's no doubt that Huberta had earned her fame — and her Royal Reward.

# "HIKING HIPPO" FOUND — KING ISSUES ROYAL DECREE

**H**uberta, the famous hippo that has been hiking through South Africa for the last three years, has been found safe and well in the beautiful Keiskama River area. This will be welcome news to Huberta's many admirers, who had feared that she may have come to harm.

Also welcome will be the remarkable news that the King has issued a Royal Decree placing Huberta under his protection. Now, by law, she cannot be hunted or harmed: a fitting reward for a great and sometimes dangerous adventure.

Huberta first came to public attention in